EDEN *miniatures*

EDEN *miniatures*

Dimensions
Heart
The Snowflake Collector
The Ice King
The Planet Walk
The Tape
Istanbul
Sedartis
Encounters
The Bournemouth & Boscombe Trilogy
Insomnia
Euphoria

DIMENSIONS

Optimist

Dimensions

First Edition

Dimensions was first published as part of *EDEN by FREI*
– a concept narrative in the here & now about the where,
the wherefore and forever at *EDENbyFREI.net*

ISBN: 978-1-64370-453-1

Optimist Books by Optimist Creations

optimistcreations.com

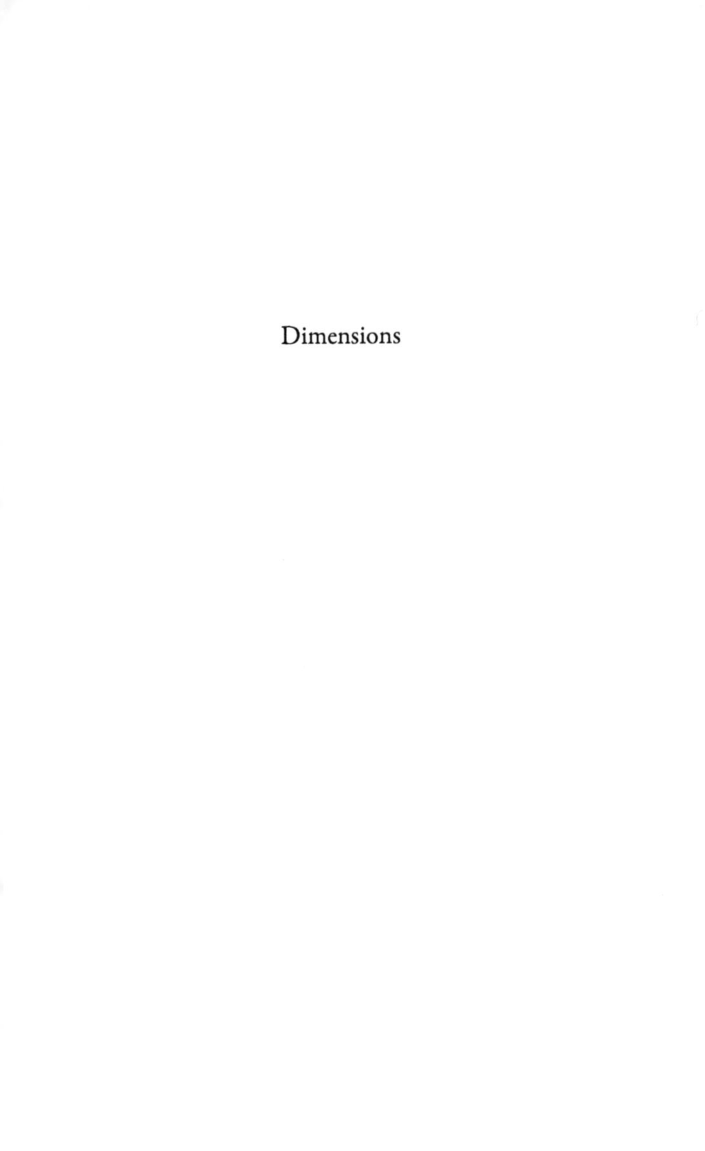

Dimensions

1 Onomatopoeia

The sound of the wheels has me
mesmerised. Decrescending upbeats
as the trains slow da-down da-down
to a halt, and doors open following an
interminable, inexplicable, insistent though
surely unnecessary delay during which
everybody waits, and the impatient poke at
unilluminated buttons.

A woman with a violent birds' nest for hair
waddles past me wafting a scent of female
exuberance right up my nostrils. Reluctant,
I inhale. A humming headache from the
night before sharpens into a short sting
of pain; doors close, the carriage yields to
a lethargic tug of tucked-away engines.
Impertinent red: this train is altogether
too colourful for this time of morning.

I have new hairs on my belly. Whatever for. Hairs on my ears too, and unruly nostrils. My body makes a mockery of me. The train now approaching platform eleven is the 08:16 South Western service to Guildford, calling at. From neighbouring platforms their own litanies of suburbia. Commuters a-coming to town to town. My eyes defocus midway round the Clapham Junction sign. I do not want to be here. The sign cares nought; it stands, proclaiming: interchange.

All passengers should change here, ideally, that would be fun. If every train that stopped here all passengers got off from and boarded another train, any other train, bound for a random destination, their daily chug would instantly cheer. Wonder whither will I today? *Uckfield?* Delightful.

The new hairs are an issue. As are the clusters of cells causing the skin to bump now, in places. My doctor reassures me they're harmless. Just keep an eye out. But these notwithstanding, and disregarding the hum in the head, which has since pitched down to an almost agreeable rumble, I feel surprisingly gruntled.

Another train, another gorge of goers to work.

I can't take my eyes off the eyes of a man hanging over a low standing station sign, talking on his mobile. Four tracks and three platforms separate us, and his hanging is most unusual: as if the sign were the stocks and he the miscreant, but nothing there to hold him firm in his trap, safe gravity, our perpetual friend. He looks straight at me but I don't think he sees me, I think he sees a giraffe or a marmot.

Perhaps more likely a kangaroo. I have never been mistaken for any of these but kangaroo likes me most, it being so resoundingly antipodean. (Which, just for clarification, I'm not.)

To my right, in the polite English morning light, a man in his twenties, in shiny grey suit trousers, jacket off, and a shirt as blue and clean as the sky. I feel like standing next to him and, putting my hand on his shoulder, inclining my head toward his collar and breathing in the warmth of his neck where his hair is tapered; folding my arm then around him and laying my hand on his chest just there by the mound of his major pectoral. But I don't, lest he take umbrage.

The 08:26 South Western service to Shepperton, calling at Earlsfield, Raynes Park, New Malden, Norbiton, Kingston,

Hampton Wick, Teddington, Fulwell, Hampton, Kempton Park, Sunbury, Upper Halliford and Shepperton. I've done it before, I can do it again. As the laggards alighting dissemble, I ease myself off my own sign post that I've been leaning against and, catching blueshirtman in profile, features untroubled by worry or strife—a young man's face of little care and littler consequence still—I board that train, godforsaken though it may be.

My destination, supposedly, on this journey, is Kingston. Not Kingston, Jamaica, but Kingston, Surrey. Upon-Thames. It is pretty in a Home Counties kind of way that elevates ordinary to a virtue and says it's all right as long as it's nice. Kingston is nice. And since Pat Val has branched out there, it's also in one pocket scrumptious. Not to mention the seven brothers from Afghanistan who set up shop here as purveyors of superfine wraps. But they didn't last long, more's the pity. After ten in the evening, in an attempt at making things just ever so slightly more cumbersome than strictly required, the station master shuts the entrance, and you have to go looking for a side door, hidden some twenty yards down the road. There's a market in the morning, and the flatspoken barista girl at Costa aims to bewilder with an unreasonable array of options for your morning coffee, and fairly succeeds. Nay, Kingston is not unusual.

The fact that I fall asleep on the train can easily be explained. The fact that I wake up on the Bosporus maybe less so. But you breakfast where you rise, and it is not for me at this moment to challenge that principle any more than to question the logic that claims to govern geometry or time, so I follow my instinct down a steep alley not far from the Swedish and French embassies, retracing my steps as best I can to an oasis of friendship I remember, as in a dream, the Limonlu Bahçe, a garden of peace.

2 The Sultaness

Shaped like a pear, she sits on the bed,
doing make-up. Her skin is coffee-coloured
soft, her eyes smile with secret knowledge,
ancient and wise. She is twenty. Unrushed
and unhurried she dabs the powder
brush to her cheek; her legs folded. Her
voluptuousness is contagious. In her lower
lip, a golden ring. She looks like a goddess,
and when she gets up, her vast midriff and
buttocks bounce to the stoic rhythm of her
stately gait. Gracious and large, she beams
life into whatever sphere encompasses her.
Gorgeous is she.

I remember her, as I look up at the waitress
who is taking my order, who by contrast
is gamine and lean and angular too. I
appreciate her angularity more than I like
it but then angular, so am I: assembled in

the right way we two could make quite a pattern. But I am seated at a table on my own, still puzzled as to why I am here, and she with her dark brown eyes and dark brown hair makes me feel I belong here. (I have pale blue eyes and no hair to speak of, except in places where it flummoxes now and perturbs me.) I order a Turkish coffee and fresh lemon juice, and I'm given a moment to look at the menu and decide what to eat. I am ravenous which makes me think I maybe haven't eaten in a while. How long does it take to get from Clapham Junction to Beyoğlu? I suppose it depends on the route.

My rational mind tells me there can be no Sultaness. Then again, my rational mind tells me I am in Kingston, Surrey. Upon the old river Thames. (It pleases me to call it 'the old river', though in truth it is unlikely to be older than most.) My rational mind is being irrelevant, I decide, and I order a hamburger with chips, because I am hungry and I don't remember being a vegetarian, though it wouldn't surprise me to find that I was. The Sultaness speaks to me now in perfectly formed elliptical syllables, and she says: 'Nearly time to make our grand entrance.' I understand her not. I'm trying to remember the night before in the hope that this would lead to something: ideally some sort of explanation, or if not that then perhaps just a shimmer of clarity.

The night before is a blur. I'd come back from Ibiza. I'd been playing water polo at three in the morning with some hearty Scandinavians in the pool. That much is certain. From then on in, nothing much is. I wonder where I'll be staying tonight, but my burger arrives and puts on hold questions and queries alike.

"Our grand entrance," she'd said. Are we in this together? I wonder have I still got my phone and I feel for it in my pocket, and there it is, no missed calls. No voicemail. No text. None new, that is, I'm not friendless. *Friends!* I could phone up a friend, I could call Michael or Richard or David or Sam and say: hey how is it going, what are you up to, have you any idea what I might be doing in Istanbul? My rational mind says that that's the way forward, but having relegated my rational mind just a moment ago I feel sheepish putting it back in charge so inelegantly so soon, and I ask for some mustard instead.

The agency hasn't rung to find out where I am. Maybe they sent me here? Unlikely, and also: what for. The fact that the agency hasn't rung to ask how long I'd be before pitching up, allowing, one imagines, a note of disapproval in their voice at having to chase me rather than me informing them of my delay due to a detour via, erm, Turkey, bodes well and ill simultaneously and in measure that broadly compares.

If they don't miss me, then I'm not in trouble for not showing up. On the other hand, if they don't miss me, perhaps I have ceased to exist? Maybe I have never existed at all and am no more and no less than a figment of my imagination. I like the word *figment* and decide to use it again soon, but unpaired from 'imagination' to make it thus more particular, to me. The agency hasn't phoned and it's now what, coming up to eleven, but Turkey is two hours ahead, so that could mean that they might phone any moment; maybe I should call them right now. Or would that be overhasty, even drastic. Maybe the agency too has ceased to exist, or has never existed at all and is in fact no more and no less than a figment of its own imagination. (Ah yes, I walked right into that one.)

I notice that I have not run out of cigarettes and decide to allow myself one now, as the circumstances are clearly extenuating. The ritual of lighting it, the sensation of pulling in the warm air. The exhaling, with a lower jaw jutted out just ever so slightly. What obfuscates the atmosphere may yet purge the mind. My headache has gone, that's a relief.

{Reflexion}

Old spellings. I like them. Archaic turns of phrase. Askewnesses, plurals. The Thisness and Thatness of it All: attributation, verbing & nouns. The Ampersand.

I like my reality. It's not as if I'm married to it, I haven't sworn allegiance to it, and it not to me, we are not, in that sense, committed to each other, nor in any other sense, I believe. But having been together coming up half a century, I paddle in the comfort of its familiarity, as in a hot tub that isn't quite hot, merely warm. We do, I feel, know each other. So naturally, *naturally,* I'm irked when it deserts me; not upset, I don't upset easily, nor do I anger; hardly at all.

Rhythmic repetitions. Is Y a consonant or a vowel, and why. Eschewing question marks.

Conundra.

3 Memories of the Future: A Leak and the Edgy Etonian

In the great scheme of things—and I like the expression 'great scheme of things': it suggests both that there is a scheme to begin with, and that it is great—my disorientation of this Tuesday morning is not grave. It is still Tuesday, I assume, though I haven't checked, but there is no reason to believe that it isn't, except perhaps for the time-space discontinuation that my being here at the Limonlu Bahçe now implies, if in fact Tuesday it still is. I boarded a train at Clapham Junction 08:26, and it is now roughly half past eleven. The burger, as expected, was delicious. I don't suffer from amnesia, at least not as far as I can remember. Ka-*ching.*

Italicising.

One word paragraphs. Short sentences, more so still long.

What confounds me is a memory of the future; I'm aware it's a memory because that's what it feels like and it's how it constructs itself, in layers, like a relief or part of a sculpture that has age-old dust cautiously blown or brushed off it, and I'm certain it's of the future because I have no recollection of it in the past, and since I'm not suffering from amnesia I would know if I had.

There's a leak making itself known in my neighbour's ceiling which has not been explained. It's been there for a week now and it first showed itself last Sunday when I wasn't even at home, I was in Cornwall. I received a message from my neighbour who lives in the flat below me, saying there is a leak, could I check; I texted back, saying I'm on the road right now but if it's urgent, he should let himself in (providence: I'd pressed a set of keys to my flat into his hand the first time I met him, in case of emergency). He texted me back once again, saying that this was not an emergency and it could wait until I got back, since the stain on his ceiling was quite small and not growing bigger.

Three days later, on Wednesday, Peppe the builder who's from near Pompeii (where, he tells me, the Mafia is) comes in and has a look around and is hardly perturbed. It's not, he assures me, coming from my shower, and not from my sink. It might be coming from some old pipe between my floor and my neighbour's ceiling, but it could also be from an unproof spot in the wall, possibly where there's a ledge. The building is a hundred years old, after all:

we should wait and see. Another three days pass (plus the Wednesday, makes seven in total so far), and again on a Sunday, my neighbour phones me up to tell me the stain has now grown, quite a bit. There has been no rain. I have not been doing anything untoward or unusual since last night, at least not that I can recall, and my recall of events, as has been established, remains intact.

I say intact. I have a terrible memory, if truth be told, and truth be told. What's the point of telling anything, if it isn't, essentially, true. Both the leak and the young man who's been to Eton have not yet occurred, at least not to me, but I remember them clearly, I remember the leak more clearly than I remember the young man, because he appeared after several drinks at a bar and he sounded unfeasibly posh. He said so himself: "I just sound unfeasibly posh," is what he said. And he did sound unfeasibly posh, it was most incongruous. He was wearing a hoodie-kind top, though it may or may not have actually had a hood, and he was worried about losing his hair. His hair looked fine to me, but then I lost mine at his age, so perhaps I'm just used to the concept of early onset alopecia; apparently it's genetic.

He fretted about sounding too posh to get girls and professed that he much preferred the company of gay men because they were funnier, he thought, than straight people in general, and he was losing hair over losing his hair—which to me seemed unfortunate as well as unnecessary—and he was dressing down so as to mask the unfeasible poshness of his voice. I liked him immediately, but he got into an argument with my friend whom I was out with that night, even though I told them both to be nice to each other, and later on they did the same thing again. That was a curious evening. I'd already been chatted up thrice by three women, four times if you count the one who came up to me twice. That doesn't usually happen: I must have signalled approachability.

The young man who'd been to Eton had a gay dad and a gay godfather. And he was rather too fond, I got the impression, of coke. He offered me a tiny bit from a practically empty sachet that he took from his wallet, scooped up onto the rounded corner of his payment card, which means I must have read his name, but that didn't register. The instant dislike that my friend had taken to him was now getting stronger. The young Etonian whose name I may have read but which did not lodge itself in my mind, at least not consciously, asked if I wanted to get some more and I said I wouldn't know where or how but in essence why not (I'd had rather more than one or two drinks...) and he said he could get some straight away, but we couldn't, for reasons I didn't quite understand, go to his place for this, even though it was just round the corner. I didn't think it wise or even just comfortable to stay where we were and do Class A drugs right under the noses of the bouncers, literally on the pavement, and also I didn't have, nor did I want to spend, any money.

We left it at that and at one point the bouncers ushered us inside (it was coming up three in the morning) and the young man came back and asked us for a pound to get home but I genuinely didn't have a pound on me, I had been paying by card all night long, and my friend didn't like him, so he didn't give him a pound, and then the young man showed his edge a bit and started abusing my friend, but I couldn't hear what he was saying because the music in there was too loud, and my friend looked perturbed but took it all in calm resignation, as if that were just the kind of thing that normally happens at the end of an evening, unpleasant though it may be; and that, I thought, was that. Except once we were outside, the Edgy Etonian suddenly materialised again and I asked him what he'd said to my friend and he apologised, saying he'd got carried away a bit, or words to that effect, and my friend left and I said goodbye to the stranger who had nearly been pleasant enough a random encounter to become a friend too, but had now rather spoilt it, and I worried about my friend because he'd looked so dejected and also he had to get back to Earlsfield, which is right in the middle of technically nowhere, especially if you're travelling after three in the morning.

None of this particularly fits anywhere, I realise, but I remember it as I sit here in this garden of civilised repose, in one of the trendier portions of Istanbul. Except none of it has yet occurred, it was all yet to come.

I check my phone. No, it is still Tuesday, coming up noon. High time, I sense, although with a crushing vagueness as to what this might mean, to 'get going'. I order a Bloody Mary.

4 The Sultaness (Reclining)

The Sultaness sleeps like a Matisse Nude,
a duvet draped over one leg only, casually
veiling the sanctity of her majestic vagina.
Her arm stretched out over the edge of
the mattress, her head inclined tward the
window whence barely a breeze now teases
the heat of the afternoon, not quite away.

I marvel at her voluminous undulations.
How did she get here? Into the
imaginarium of my mind, into my
brainspace, my own private place of
precious wonder?

My Bloody Mary arrives from the creature
who reminds me of her as well as of me,
and I confer upon myself the privilege
of some measured doubt. I could be
dreaming: I could be asleep still on the

train to Kingston and wake up any moment now, quite possibly with a hard on. I am not normally given to arousal by women, round-shaped or angular, but hey, if this is a dream then anything might happen. Might it not.

The thought of quite possibly still being asleep reassures me for the time-being, as does the Mary which is Bloody and perfect and has enough of a kick to it to feel real: I begin to relax.

5 Youth

Talking to the man who doesn't need to shave fills in me a well of melancholy, sudden and post conversation. The conversation features the most delightful frog in short film history (yet to be made), among many other things that give me mirth and pleasure, not least looking into his silvery eyes. Unlike most other young men of an age at which they don't have to shave, he holds my gaze, steady as a hypnotist. His eyes are memorably shaped, as if they were placed in his face upside down, just a little. Silvery grey.

The sadness sets in after I've left the party at which we spend a couple of hours or so talking as the sun goes down over the back garden. It's more of a backyard than an actual garden, with wild grass growing all over and a neighbour's dog actually digging up his there hidden bones. I'd never seen that before, other than in comics (and I'm not an avid fan or consumer of comics, haven't been since I was about twelve). It's not his youth that brings on my deep sorrow verging on despair, nor anything he said nor the fact that he is bright and well spoken, nor let alone that he doesn't seem to need to shave. I reckon I must be close to twice his age but luckily not as old as his dad. His dad sounds ancient and excellent, formidable in one field or another. By age though, I could be his dad. This casts a pall of umbra over my otherwise sanguine disposition.

I know! I'm having my midlife crisis. It's plain and perhaps just tadwise banal. I am projecting my discomfiture with the impending calamity of fifty onto the part of my mind that clings on to diversion for dear life. I make believe. The irksomeness of my situation begins to creep up on me, like a nebulous mist. (Tautology.) I have made it to midpoint completely unnoticed: I am invisible to the naked eye. And the next few days will have been cataclysmic, so small wonder I'm having an existential wobble. But the good thing is that this time I did not fall in love: not with my friend on the South Bank (though that would have been easy), not with the young man who doesn't need to shave. (Easier still.) Most certainly not with Poshvoiced Hoodie and, no, not with the man in a blue shirt at Clapham Junction, should you wonder. (Have you ever noticed how many sprucely scrubbed men, tender in years and wearing ironed blue shirts, stand at any given station on any commutable morning... – It's a rhetorical question?)

As well as being unfamous, I am also perennially poor. My chosen path of professional endeavour has so far yielded no hint of a fortune. This has the advantage that I remain unencumbered, I suppose, by wealth's weight: what I don't have I can't lose, and I know more than I care to cerebrate that the things I own own me quite as much. Take my laptop for instance: without it I am nought. I have dislodged myself to the continent's end, but my Mac is still here: I find that reassuring.

I will the straw in my drink to suck up one more residual sip of tomato juice laced with vodka, and it complies with a gurgling sound, which attracts the attention of a boy sitting two tables removed. He gives me a look of aloof disdain, and in his eyes, which are the colour of mine, I detect a familiar glint that I cannot put name nor nature to, no. He seems to consider disapproving of me but stops short of a sneer, and his very fine lips instead curl into almost a smile. I'm so surprised at this, I put down my glass and smile back at him, which changes his demeanour to a tinge of distaste.

He, much like the young man who does not need to shave and whom I am yet to meet, has no facial growth, and his lightly tan skin looks fluffdown soft. He appears as out of place here as I do, and quite as at home. Wherein lies a paradox that tickles me and I catch myself grinning just to myself.

The boy lets a few moments pass in contemplation of his plate on which there appears to have been a kebab or salad, as if to decide whether or not he should scrape the remnants of whatever it was with his fork or knife or even fingers (though he doesn't strike me as the kind of person who, given the choice, would use his fingers to scrape up anything, let alone food); or maybe he's versed in the mystical art of reading the scraps. As far as I can tell from where I'm sitting (and without ungainlily craning my neck) it looks unlikely that the plate is going to yield up much insight. He appears to come to that same conclusion himself and now looks up, but not at me or at anyone in particular, but into the generality of the world straight ahead, a little bemused and distracted.

I feel like I know him already but clearly I don't. I have no idea. I have a looming sense of foreboding.

6 Descending, Temporarily, Into the Unrequired Sludge of Unrequited (at Least to Reciprocal Level) Affection, Again

This happens so regularly, so predictably, I should be inured to it.

I am not.

As if he'd read my mind, the man who doesn't need to shave, on our second meeting, wears the tiniest hint of stubble. He has spent the night in Peckham, but does not volunteer any more details about why or with whom. My impression is that it was a simple case of crashing at a mate's house, but that impression may just be wrong. I don't feel I know him well enough to enquire about this or the number of days he hasn't shaved, so I can't tell whether this is just the result of one night's morning's not shaving, or whether it is in fact the protrusion of several days. Faint though it is, it nevertheless intrigues me because it comes up so different to the soft light blond tuft that sits off the lower side of his jaw bone and the two or three long hairs that sprout from his little mole near the back of his cheek. The 'stubble', such as it is, shows up in short little thick pins, which compared to the rest of his head appear black.

We sit opposite each other, discussing comedy, I believe, though my mind is only half on it. The other half of my mind—my conscious mind, we're always talking about, I have far less of a hold, if any, on my subconscious mind, if that isn't plainly stating the obvious, which plainly it is—is divided into roughly four areas of attention, each approximately equal in measure: one quarter takes in the astonishing, familiar, but nevertheless new-from-this-angle scenery, on the Dove's terrace, with Turner clouds in the sky and rowers already back on the river; another quarter takes in the mild tea taste of the light ale my fellow drinker has bought for our second round and that he'd described, after the first sip, as "undeniably unusual but not altogether unpleasant;" a third quarter has registered that the Turner clouds have now once more wholly obscured the sun and I can take off my sunglasses again which I do think is kinder on the person sitting opposite; and the fourth quarter is taking in the person sitting opposite, thinking: you are exactly the kind I would fall in love with, but I won't, except that I will, and if truth be told—*and it be!*—I already am. Falling. 'Falling' is maybe not the right word: sinking, more like. Slowly, as into quicksand. Calamitous, and thrilling. Degrounding, inexorably (or is that just a *cliché*), in... *love?*

Perhaps not, perhaps that would be not only insane but also a further distortion of not just the heart and the mind and the soul but most inexcusably of the truth; and truth, we have already exclaimed, *be told!* A glow of untenable, unsustainable, inexplicable, unwarranted, but oh in life indispensable warmth that says: I like you. More than makes any sense. It will pass. It will solidify, the ground. Mush will turn into dependable clay, on which to build.

There will be friendship and love there will be friendship and love, and the two will and will not be the same.

Far be it from me to claim that I can't say I'm not entirely impartial to the occasional quadruple negative...

{Meander}

The strident thrust of a century recently launched, and with great fanfare too. Millennium. Nobody talks about that, no more. (A comma makes all the difference.)

There are aeroplanes flying overhead there are cars on the road there are people in the street about town. Forward motion, always. It likes me not; not always, not now. I long to ease. Not from now on, just for right now. Much needs to be done, but it's good to do nothing, once in a while; just to float. Relent to slow the flow of time. Be. Not go anywhere. At all. Except you always do, don't you. You can sit in a spot for eternity and when eternity is over you will have moved. Away from the centre, along the Milky Way, around the star, on your planet's axis, many times.

Once upon a time in a story I knew this to be true and I said so and I said it was disconcerting, but nonetheless comforting, too. And it was. And it is.

Then a kiss.

7 Love

Being invisible to the naked eye has the advantage that you can watch and learn.

I sit on a tube train wearing a hat, and I examine the people sitting across from me. Nobody notices, nobody minds. I love looking at people. I love people. I love. I've put half a century on the clock and not ever experienced *'love',* not *love in return,* not *'I love you,' 'I love you too'* love. I *feel* love all the time, I gush all aglow at the slightest appearance of beauty or kindness or both or even just quirky adorableness, and I forever fascinate at the troubled soul. But never has anyone whom I felt myself as 'in love with' felt that way about me. Or vice versa. That is strange. As it so seems the norm. Then again, I've never subscribed to 'the norm'.

Back at the Limonlu Bahçe, the boy's sun bleached hair is lighter blond than it would be had he not spent some time on the beach, I assume. I feel like talking to him, but I don't know what to say. And I don't want to scare him; I remember what I was like when I was that age, and although I was fiercely independent and unselfconsciously 'cool', I was also wary of men of the age I am now. They were *ancient.* And really what was their point.

I put myself in his place and imagine myself looking at me from where he's sitting, still held in a momentary trance, and I find it surprisingly easy to see what he sees and feel what he feels and know what he knows and be what he is and it hits me: I'm he.

Not metaphorically speaking in a similarity kind of way vaguely so, but for real. No wonder he looks so familiar. And so abjectly alien too. I have manoeuvred myself into a space-time-convolution in which for reasons I cannot begin to imagine I am sitting twelve feet away from myself, some twenty-eight years removed. Holy cow.

8 The Leopard (and His Spots)

We're into weird territory now, and I'm a little excited. My hold on reality—loose as it's been (so as not to say non-existent) since early this morning—has just undergone one more lateral nudge. Whatever I'm clasping at now is clearly not what I'm used to. I can't blame the Bloody Mary: it may have been perfect, but it was not nearly so strong as to give me hallucinations. Do Bloody Marys ever? Is seeing yourself as a youthful rendering in your current day environment a hallucination? Then again, is a somewhat trendy garden bar cafe restaurant in the currently fashionable part of Istanbul 'my environment'? And what are they thinking of me in Kingston, Surrey, right now? Should I care?

I resolve, for the first time really today, to 'deal' with the situation. Right up until now, I have been essentially bewildered and in no small measure bemused by my overall predicament, but now it transpires there's something I must do. This fills me with gloom quite as much as it stirs me. Ideally, I would do nothing. I would sit here and wait for it all—whatever 'it' is—to just go away. But conditions are no longer ideal. Whereas until a few minutes ago I was maybe disorientated but principally happy to just exist in a reality that didn't quite make sense but that would probably, I surmised, explain itself to me in one way or another sooner or later, I am now deeply discomfited. And as the extraordinariness of my state begins to dawn on me, it also begins to impose itself on me with a meaning, a forceful declamation of purpose: it seems to be saying, you are here *precisely* to confront your own younger self. And that is plainly absurd.

The angular waitress is nowhere to be seen and so I halfheartedly wave at a sweet looking colleague of hers who is and has been all smiles. He looks about twenty-seven-and-three-and-a-half-months and wears one discreet earring and a handsome tattoo that encircles his arm below a deliberately high-rolled shirt sleeve. He likes me, I think, but then at the moment I am quite likeable, and quite helpless, as I glance up at him and ask him what it was that the young man over there had eaten, offering him an innocent smile: before you interfere with your reality, check it.

He glances halfway over his shoulder and furrows his brow for an instant or two, and my heart sinks. There's nobody there. I'm imagining him, I am losing control. Hah, losing control, I've lost it several hours ago, possibly several decades...

He slowly turns back to me and declares: 'Kebab. Mixed kebab and salad. Are you still hungry?' – 'No,' I reply, only now aware of how odd a question that must have seemed, 'no, not at all, I was just wondering; it looked nice.' This satisfies him, and from his expectant look I deduce that he thinks I will want to order something anyway, maybe another coffee? I pause for a moment and then say, as if that was the most natural thing in the world: 'do you think he would mind if I asked him a question?'

Ahmed—I later find out is his name—cocks his head a bit as if to say 'are you serious?' but instead, with a still growing smile says: 'There is no harm in asking a question.' I am relieved, but not sure that he's right, necessarily. Would that not depend on the question?

I feel I have caught myself on the hop and I order, somewhat on a whim, a mojito this time round and—sensing my window of opportunity close and the boldness in my adrenalin-fuelled heart wane—ask Ahmed to ask young me (without referring to him as young me, for obvious reasons) if he would join me for one, as I would like to, there being no harm in asking a question, ask him a question.

Ahmed seems to enjoy this task, one he has never, I fancy, been given before, and brazenly marches up to young me and asks me if I would care to join the gentleman over there for a mojito. To my unending surprise I say yes. But then I have always been good for a new conversation, even back then, when I was, or believe to remember being, naturally disposed towards caution.

As I sit there watching myself saunter over to me, I sense an overpowering surge of affection and care. God, I think to myself, if only I knew...

{Vibe}

What kind of a consciousness is it that knows itself to exist but doesn't know why? In what way does that make sense? In what way does it not?

The quest.

The longing to learn.

The yearning for answers.

The learning to yield. If only my brain were better at retaining information. What is 'information'? And when it is not 'information', what is it then, that we get, if we get it, at all? What, if anything, can be known, can be felt, can be appreciated, understood, can be experienced or imagined, or both? And is there, but *is* there a difference?

Remembrance of things past and future. The energy stream, and the particles. Obviously, the waves. The idiosyncrasies. Material flaws. Cracks that let the light shine through. Nonuniform irregularities.

Quantum behaviour...

9 Memories of the Future and of the Past: Walks on Water

Linearity, unhinged. The flashforwards keep coming: not premonitions. Memories of things that haven't yet happened. I have no explanation other than that I've stepped outwith the continuum, I know not how. Time and space disjointed. Perhaps that's what comes from not taking either too seriously, ever.

I walk through the snow in Kensington Gardens: about three inches of a softish sluggish powdery white that has its own decorative whimsy, now that it is sodden and trodden through. People have spent the weekend rolling snow balls and leaving them dotted around the park. Plus the occasional snowman. Mostly though only accumulations of snow the approximate size of an average snowman's rump.

I wander and ponder my diagonal position in life. I use too many words, I am told. Frequently. All the time. Words words words words words words words. I use seven when one would do. But would one *do?* Would one word, would one word do? Would it now. And would it do what? And for whom? And says who? Rhythms and patterns. And repetitions. Nobody likes them as much as I do, it seems. Relishing words, for the love of words, words in their own right, to no end and no purpose, propelling no plot, describing no thing, put there for their very own sake. Superfluousness:

Abundance.

Words for what they are, not what they're worth. A picture paints a thousand words; a word, when pictures in their thousands fail, may say it all. Nobody gets that. It follows that nobody gets me: I am my words, that's what I am, they are me.

I'm little else, nothing. Else. Really. I am *obviously* not my body. The ways in which I neglect my body are subtle, I don't actively abuse it. I don't damage it, or only slightly, sometimes, and not wantonly. I'm not vain, though I am, I perceive, as I tangent the bedecked lawn with its broad traces of snowballing on it, a tad narcissistic. I don't *want* to be, but I am a little in love with myself. Damn, another unwelcome insight. But I have to be a little in love with myself: I'm single and somewhat singular. If I don't love me at least a little then nobody loves me at all and that would be heartbreaking, sad. The differential between lone and lonesome; lonely, alone. Now that I know I am troubled, troubled I see that nobody knows the trouble I see. In all likelihood it is true: I do have a bit of a Messiah complex as well, but then so did Jesus.

I remember walking through the snow in Kensington Gardens once before, though there wasn't as much then, snow. There was ice, however, on the Round Pond, and my girlfriend—my girl friend, then girlfriend—and I came up towards it in deep conversation, and we liked the idea of walking on ice, it was a London park in January thing to do, and I was new to London in January and she was visiting me and we tested the ice just a bit and found it sufficiently strong and so we started crossing the pond. There was magic abroad in the air, or would have been, had I felt towards her quite as she did towards me.

She was, I believe, in love with me, deeply. I liked her. And found her likeable and attractive as a human being but I wasn't 'attracted' to her. We came to the middle of the pond and looked around and enjoyed the ducks and the geese being clumsy, and then we walked on, and shortly before we reached the other side we happened upon a sign that said "DANGER THIN ICE" and we laughed and we came off the ice and continued our walk, talking.

That's how young we were, how unencumbered. I'm a little in love with that boy, that lad, that young man. I was never really a lad, I don't think, I was hardly ever a boy, I was a very young man though. I certainly was never a *guy* or a *geezer*. I was earnest and a little pretentious, in fairness; maybe a lot. And possibly just on the borderline end of marginally autistic; maybe just eligible, by today's standards, for on-the-scale Asperger's, though of that I can't now be sure.

And now I know that within seconds I'll be sitting opposite him, that exact young man, of exactly that age, who still, I imagine, thinks of that girl as his girlfriend, even though he already knows he can't love her, not in the way she loves him. Shall I tell him? And if I tell him, shall I tell him also not to walk on the ice, as it's nowhere near thick enough and he and his girl friend might die? That would be the responsible thing to do, surely, to *warn* him. After all, this isn't just about me any more, this is also about her! Imagine how I would feel today if we'd crashed into the water in Kensington Gardens and both of us had drowned. Or worse still, if I had survived, so I could feel something, anything at all, today, but she had drowned, and try as I might I could not save her?

My heart feels a jolt of guilt and remorse at not having saved her, though sincerely I tried, when I remember that we walked off that ice and laughed. And that laughter I remember completely. That is a memory of the past. It is real and proper and warm and good. We were a little in love with each other, perhaps, after all. That laughter, that unencumberedness. That not looking back on the ice in horror to check how thin was it really, that just walking on. Hand in hand. Laughing. I love him for that, I love her for it too.

He wanders over, languid, slow, and sits down at my table, at a right angle from me, with a tentative smile: it's most familiar this, this *almost* smile, this nearly-a-smile-but-not-quite, with an almost glint in his eye, but also a question.

He is frank, but not so frank as to be forward, his mind is open, just as mine was when I was him, but also naturally cautious. I don't remember this scene, this encounter from my youth at all, which makes me think that maybe this is a complete stranger and I'm projecting onto him my own invention of a version of my youth; and, seeing that I've lost my grip on continuity and the concordance of time and space with no possible explanation for how it is that I'm in Istanbul, none of this would surprise me.

'Hello...'—he looks at me as if he registered something from his own future or his own past (though that, too, may well just be in my mind), but he doesn't recognise me, I'm glad: it was brazen of me to ask him over; I could ruin everything. What, though, is 'everything'?—'...I'm George.'

I want to say: 'I know,' but that would be certain to confuse him.

'Good to meet you George, my name is Sebastian.'

He gives me another frank look with an almost-smile that this time round might just tip over into a grin, a benign one, but it doesn't; instead his face settles into a look that says: you interest me and that alone is worth something, go on then.

I'm in. I don't know what I'm in, or in for, but I can tell from his unjaded eyes that he likes the curiosity of this situation. He likes curiosity, and he's not scared. He never was scared, I think, as I watch him look up at Ahmed who returns with our mojitos. He likes Ahmed, he finds him attractive. Can you blame him. Ahmed thinks nothing of it and smiles at us both, in almost equal measure, though I sense a nod more towards me than my younger self George, but maybe I flatter myself thinking so, and also I know what I was like then, I was incapable of flirtation. Nowadays I just surrender.

How to proceed? Am I going to tell George: look at me, I am what will become of you. That would be insane.

And horrendously cruel, surely: what if he doesn't want to look his self-to-be in they eye, at this particular juncture, right here and now and without warning or opportunity to think about it, what if he just wants to have a mojito with an oddly familiar seeming stranger twice his age, and maybe hear something about the world that nobody's ever told him?

Nor, clearly, am I going to tell George my life story, the twenty-eight years or so that will constitute the distance between him and me. That would be simply unfair, and take forever.

So what *am* I going to tell him? Ask him? Want of him? For a brief but potentially panic-inducing moment it occurs to me that if we were to get on so well as to decide, maybe after a few cocktails or so, to go for a walk and then maybe dinner and then his hotel (seeing that I haven't got one), I could end up quite conceivably in an intimate encounter with myself, in the most unorthodox way. That would be taking things way too far, I decide, and resolve to not let it come to this *under any circumstances:* this one mojito, that's it. (What *are* our circumstances, I continue to wonder...) He raises his glass and offers me cheers. I let that thought go and return the compliment.

The mojito—much as the Bloody Mary had been—is near perfect with an appreciable kick to it, and I further resolve not to resolve anything more for the time-being and instead allow myself simply to be there *in* that moment and see what next might unfold...

11 Death (Imagined)

I noticed I was dead when I saw myself lying dead in my bed, looking down on myself from a great height: there I was. Gone. A lifelong flirtation with significance, over. And nothing dreadful in consequence. No pain, no loss, no uncertainty. Just the remorseless ease of an expired existence. Of almost failure. Of having nearly been. Something or other. Someone? Then I woke up and realised that it had been a dream. I don't like to say 'only', but it had been 'only' a dream. I had dreamt my self dead. What new joys. Wait on me.

It's hard now to say what perplexed me more. Being dead (in my dream), or being alive (after all). But finding myself thus among the quick in a hitherto slow existence, I believed I had heard, and was minded to heed, a call for action: I got out of bed and made coffee.

Mug in hand I stood in front of the bathroom mirror, naked. I do that a lot these days, I examine my body. I marvel at it, not admiringly: bemused. I don't look for blemishes or signs of decay, I look for signs of familiarity; for something that says: this is you. I don't find it. The person standing naked in the mirror in front of me could be anybody. It's not that I'm alien to myself or strange, just: unfamiliar. I'm roughly fifty and not beautiful. What I marvel at is not beauty. What I marvel at is the fact that I don't recognise myself in the shape I've become. I'm not even unattractive. In fact, I may be more attractive now than I've ever been. And I'm not even sure if that's a good thing or a bad thing. I'm not sure it's a thing. Any more.

'Attractive'. To what and to whom and to what end. Nevertheless, I'm a little alarmed because it seems late in the day to suddenly start feeling attractive. Alarmed but a little reassured too, because perhaps it just means I'm not over the hill. What is the hill? Going down is supposed to be easier than going up. What ride am I in for? Now?

Mug in hand I stand in front of the mirror naked, looking for signs of familiarity. The eyes maybe. Or the nose. Maybe the lips. I'm stubbly, and I like it. There. That's something to hold on to: seeing as it is that I'm alive, there's one thing that I'm happy with and that's worth holding on to: my stubble.

I remind myself I am sitting opposite my young self and I had promised my young self—not so much promised, perhaps, as enticed him over by means of the prospect of—a question. My mind goes blank. The memory of imagining my own death, even just as a dream, and the image of my standing in front of the mirror naked, mug in hand and content that I have inexplicably become 'attractive', possibly owing to stubble (which has since grown somewhat into a near-mature beard), sends a shudder down my spine, and I put down my mojito too firmly.

'George,' I say, sensing that something—anything—is required from me at this point, 'what are you doing in Istanbul?'

This is not, obviously, the question I'd had in mind for him, but then I can't begin to conceive of what question I might have had in mind for him, and since it's a question that is playing on my mind about myself (what *am I* doing in Istanbul?) I feel it is pertinent, or if not pertinent then perhaps justified, or if not justified then at least maybe useful, useful in as much at least as it might open the conversation; and at this point in the proceedings (*are* these 'proceedings', and if so what are they?) I yearn for a touch of conversation.

I startle myself at realising I also yearn for a touch, his touch, any touch, some contact beyond verbal, visual, aural, and I want to place my hand over his in a fatherly gesture. I don't. But there are now two versions of us sitting at this table in the garden of the Limonlu Bahçe: one, the 'real' one, in which he still holds his glass in both his hands and has his eyes not exactly fixed but nevertheless on it, whereas I look at him in my ongoing state of bewilderment, and one, the 'imagined' one in my mind, where he has put down his glass and I have cupped my left hand over both his hands and I look him in the eyes and he looks back into mine.

'Not exactly sure,' he says—in one version examining the glass in his hands and twisting it slightly, in the other holding my gaze with a blend of confidence and the uncertainty his words imply—'I was doing *Interrail* with a friend, I had no intention of coming here really, but maybe circumstances conspired...'

I know at once that they did, even though I still don't remember this scene from my past, and I am immeasurably relieved; he is, although he doesn't know it, similarly displaced from his own reality: we are on the same page, more or less.

I imagine squeezing his hand and cupping my right hand around his neck and pulling him close so he can rest his head for a while on my shoulder, but instead I pick up my glass and lift it up to him and say, as if I had any authority to do so: 'welcome to Istanbul,' to which, in both versions, he too raises his glass and clinks it with mine and, once again gamely, says: 'welcome to Istanbul.'

12 The Sultaness (Revisited)

She doesn't leave me alone, this woman, plausibly because she's so womanly. With a regrettable paucity of experience, I retain an abstract notion at best of what Woman is. Or Man, coming to think of it. In all likelihood and compared to most, I retain a largely abstract notion of what anyone is. Are we human? Or are we dancer.

I imagine her on a mountain of cushions, brushing her hair. A dwarf eunuch wafting air upon her with a Pergamon fan. As I enter the room—is it a hall, a tent, a *boudoir?*—she looks up at me with an aloofness that is both superior and benign. She doesn't know who I am, and neither do I, although she has spoken to me already, in mysterious ways.

Woven into the pillows are the sorrows and tears of the virgins that were slaughtered in vain, and the hopes and aspirations of their betrothed princes, kept and murdered as slaves. I hear the din of the bazar and I smell its scents which are, as expected, exotic, and I hear the muezzin's adhan. This call I heed, though I am not a believer, and leave her waiting, once more. She knows, and stifles a yawn, but inwardly she delights.

It occurs to me that it does not matter. It matters not why The Sultaness has taken up residence in my mind any more than it matters why I have come to Istanbul to encounter my thirty-years younger self. It matters not that I make no sense to myself at the moment and it matters not that looking at George here who is me at the age of about twenty, I can't be in Kingston-upon-Thames at the same time, and it never ever mattered what I was going to go there for in the first place; or second, or third.

What matters is just that I don't get these next fifty seconds wrong. If I don't come up with a question that has at least some weight, some inquisitive purpose to it, he'll not only think me lame but he'll be bound to query my motives. And although I know and remember myself as someone who will for as long as possible give anyone the benefit of the doubt, I also know that once that bond of trust is broken it cannot be repaired, not easily; maybe never. I don't want to let myself down.

And so asking him how he is doing, or where he is from, or what he makes of this city, or where he is headed next, or how he enjoys his mojito, none of these will do (although I am in fact interested to know how his *Interrail* trip ended up landing him here on the outside edge of Europe, and what might have happened to his friend, and which friend it was, since I clearly would know him; but that also holds me at bay: I should not enquire about our mutual friend, as that mutuality, once established, would very obviously demand some explanation). Nor do I want to ask him some random question, such as what is the meaning of life, or pretend that there is some information he has that I need, or anything utilitarian, like where is a good place to eat. (Besides, we are at a good place to eat already, and I know we are both creatures of habit, so unnecessarily asking for a different place to eat would make me sound either disingenuous or stupid.)

I wait until he has taken another sip from his cocktail—only now does it really occur to me that that's what we are doing: drinking cocktails—and ask him, 'where do you imagine yourself in, say, 30 years from today.'

No sooner have I spoken these words than
I realise just how absurd this is: thirty years
from now I'll be eighty and he will be fifty;
what is he supposed to answer? Will thirty
years from now be thirty years down his
timeline, or mine? And won't that depend
on how the next fifty seconds, and then
fifty minutes and maybe then fifty hours
pan out?

I sense that my reality is about to implode,
when he does something unexpected.
Having been him, it shouldn't come
so unexpected to me; having been him
I should have seen this coming—in a
more normal situation perhaps even
remembered—but he nevertheless catches
me out and fairly floors me:
'In a place like this,' he says, laconic
and calm, with his innocence and nascent
wisdom and a curious sparkle in his eye,
'talking to someone like you...'

www.ingramcontent.com/pod-product-compliance
Ingram Content Group UK Ltd.
Pitfield, Milton Keynes, MK11 3LW, UK
UKHW041842200726
13854UKWH00005BA/1989

9 781643 704531